LET'S VISIT
A Spaghetti Factory

by Melinda Corey

photography by Donald N. Emmerich

Troll Associates

Library of Congress Cataloging-in-Publication Data

Corey, Melinda.
    Let's visit a spaghetti factory / by Melinda Corey; photography
by Donald Emmerich.
        p.   cm.
    Summary: Describes where spaghetti and other types of pasta come
from, the activities at a spaghetti factory, making pasta crafts,
and cooking with pasta.
        ISBN 0-8167-1741-9 (lib. bdg.)   ISBN 0-8167-1742-7 (pbk.)
        1. Pasta products—Juvenile literature.   [1. Pasta products.]
    I. Emmerich, Donald, ill.   II. Title.   III. Series.
    TP435.M3C67   1990
    664'.755—dc20   89-5110

The author and publisher wish to thank Elizabeth Rees; and Moira Eslinger, Susan M. Quillin, Don Litterer,
and the rest of the staff at the Creamette Company for their generous assistance. They also
gratefully acknowledge the Office of Governmental and Public Affairs of the United States Department
of Agriculture for the photographs on page 4; Nancy Coplon for the photographs on pages 15, 16, and 17;
and the Creamette Company for the photographs on page 29 and the recipe on page 31.

When it's dinner time, and you are having pasta, what kind of pasta will you have? There are so many shapes and sizes to choose from. There are round wheels, curvy shells, skinny spaghetti, and curly lasagna. Where do they all come from?

Pasta is made from *durum wheat*, which grows in big, flat wheat fields. Durum wheat stalks are tall and golden brown in color. When their kernels are *milled*, or ground, they produce *semolina* flour, which is sold to pasta companies to make spaghetti and other pasta. Let's visit a spaghetti factory and find out what happens to semolina when it is delivered there.

Every day, trains deliver tons of semolina to the factory. Each rail car contains 100,000 pounds of flour. When the factory is in full production, over two and a half rail cars full of semolina are processed into pasta each day. That's over 250,000 pounds of flour!

Before the semolina is unloaded, samples must be taken into the factory laboratory to be inspected by chemists. Technicians climb up on the boxcars to gather the samples. They take samples from every rail car by inserting a long-handled scoop into the middle of each car. Each sample is placed in a separate plastic bag and coded to show which boxcar it came from.

Inside the laboratory, the chemist uses a magnifying glass and a microscope to inspect the samples for their color and purity. The flour should be golden in color and should have only a few dark specks in it. With special machines, the chemist tests the samples for protein and moisture content. If he finds any problem with the wheat, the entire rail car will be returned to the mill.

Once the flour in the rail cars has been approved, it is transferred to the factory. A worker attaches two large hose lines linking the rail car and the factory. Two types of air pressure move the flour through the tubes. Negative air pressure—lack of air—pulls the flour on a *vacuum line* from rail car to factory. Positive air pressure in the *air line* helps to push the flour by pumping air into the boxcar.

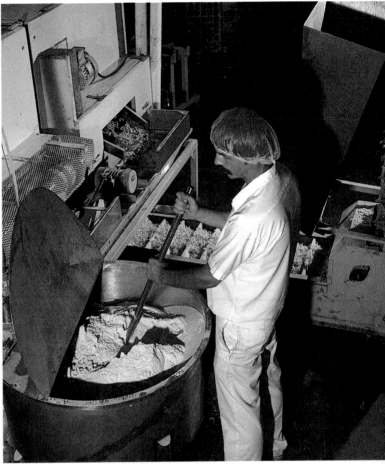

The flour is stored in giant silos inside the plant. Each silo holds 150,000 pounds of flour. To begin the 12-hour process of pasta-making, flour is transferred from the silos to the *main mixer*. There, water, semolina, and other ingredients are combined. This worker is helping to make egg noodle dough by adding powdered eggs to the flour mixture. Workers wear plastic hats to keep hair from falling into the pasta dough.

In the *vacuum mixer*, all the air is removed from the pasta dough. This process dries the pasta and eliminates air bubbles. Before the mixture enters the vacuum mixer, it contains 32% water. At the end of the process, only 12% moisture is left.

Now the pasta mixture is put into *augers*, large screwlike machines that push the dough through various *dies*, or cutters. On a wall nearby, the *panograph*, or control panel, watches over the machines in the factory. If a machine breaks down, a red light flashes, an alarm sounds, and a worker shuts the machine off.

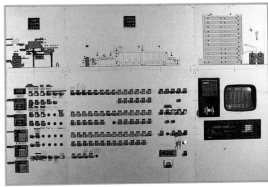

The dies are as different as the shapes of pasta they create. The die for elbow macaroni is made with hundreds of small curves to produce the familiar elbow shapes. The long rectangular die for the spaghetti is able to make many long strands of spaghetti at once.

When spaghetti comes from the *extruder*, or feeder, each double strand is about three feet long. Because the spaghetti is not yet completely dry, it is soft and limp. This bundle of freshly made spaghetti looks more like a row of yellow ribbons than something good to eat. To dry the spaghetti further, it is sent to the *pre-dryer*, which removes more of the moisture.

These lines of lasagna are also being prepared for the pre-dryer. All kinds of pasta must pass through the pre-dryer—over 4,000 pounds per hour. Next, the pasta will be moved to the *final dryer*, where even more moisture is removed. Elbows and egg noodles take only three hours to dry, while spaghetti takes as long as 10 to 12 hours.

Marathon runners often eat all kinds of pasta on the night before the race, to provide them with a good source of fuel. Pasta provides *complex carbohydrates*, which the body turns into *glycogen*, a stored fuel that provides long-lasting energy. *Simple carbohydrates*, like white sugar and most candy, provide energy, but for just a short period of time.

A light breakfast, such as toast or pancakes without syrup, provides quick energy at the start of the race. But during the race, marathon runners get most of their fuel from the complex carbohydrates they have eaten over the last few days—including the pasta they have had the night before.

The average runner stores enough glycogen for about 20 miles of running. After that, he or she runs out of this fuel. The runner then must finish the race using other, less efficient fuels stored in the body. So eating pasta the day before a race can make it easier to reach the finish line.

Back in the factory, the pasta passes through the final dryer and is now ready to be inspected. A technician examines the "curve" of elbow macaroni, as well as its color and thickness. Any pasta that does not pass this inspection is reground into flour and put through the entire pasta-making process again.

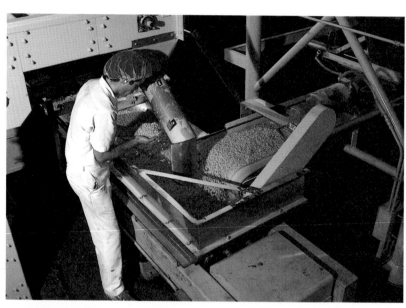

Once the elbows have been inspected and approved, they are stored in huge silos until they are packaged. Pasta of small shapes, like elbows, is packaged by machines. A feeder on the packaging machine drops one pound of elbows into an empty box. Another part of the machine closes the box. Over 200 boxes per minute are filled this way.

These mountains of egg noodles are packaged by the same kind of machinery as the elbows. They are moved on conveyor belts from their storage areas to small silos. One pound of noodles drops into a plastic bag and the machine seals the bag. At the end of the line, workers pack the bags into cartons.

Because spaghetti is more easily broken than most other pasta shapes, it requires special handling. Before it is packaged, it is stored by hanging it high above the floor. Then workers carefully watch over the machinery that measures the fragile pasta and places it into boxes. Any spaghetti that breaks or falls on the floor is sold as animal feed.

Of all pastas, lasagna requires the most delicate handling. When lasagna comes from the final dryer, a worker along the conveyor belt inspects and sorts it. Another worker divides it into one-pound portions, which are placed on metal slides. The slides drop the pasta into boxes and a machine seals the boxes. About 23 strands of lasagna fit into a one-pound box.

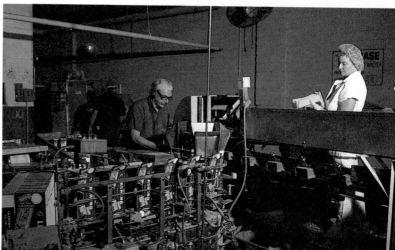

Another conveyor takes sealed cartons to the shipping area, where workers stack them on wooden platforms called *skids*. Forklift drivers move the skids of cartons to the warehouse, where they are stored until they are ready to be shipped to supermarkets.

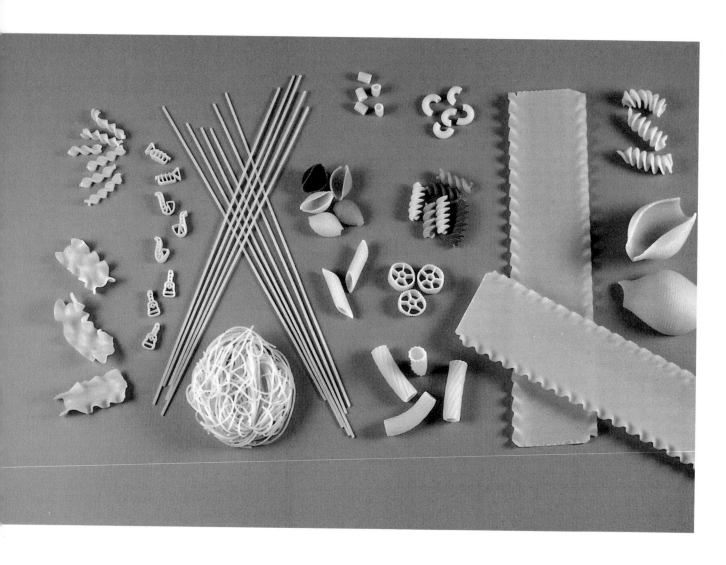

Here are just some of the types of pasta in the warehouse. Because pasta was first made in Italy, many shapes have Italian names. For example, in Italian, *spaghetti* means "little strings"; *rigatoni* means "big ridges"; *ditali* means "thimbles"; *maruzze* means "seashells"; and *capelli d'angelo* means "angel's hair."

When a supermarket places an order, workers load the cartons of pasta onto *semitrailers*, or large vans, next to the plant. Once the semi-trailers are full, drivers deliver pasta to supermarkets across the country.

At the supermarket, it's fun to choose from the rows of colorful boxes and bags of pasta. This boy wants one shape and his sister wants another. They decide to buy both, plus a few other shapes and sizes.

When they get home from the store, they have fun making some pasta crafts. First, they string together rotelle and rigatoni to make pasta necklaces. They measure the necklaces to be sure they are large enough to fit over someone's head. After each necklace is tied with a secure knot, it can be painted in bright colors.

With school glue, construction paper, and many different shapes of pasta, they create portraits of one another. Spaghetti is the best choice to show long hair, and pasta wheels make convincing eyes and ears. When the portraits are completed, it is easy to tell who is who.

Making pasta crafts is fun, but the *best* thing to do with pasta is to eat it! What will they have for dinner tonight? They think of the dishes they might make with pasta. They could make spaghetti with tomato sauce, or lasagna, or vegetable soup with spirals. It makes them hungry just to think about it.

For tonight, they decide on a macaroni salad with tuna. A parent supervises while the elbow macaroni is cooked and drained. Once the pasta is cooked, they add the tuna, vegetables, and mayonnaise. They mix everything carefully to combine the ingredients.

QUICK MACARONI SALAD

1 7-ounce package elbow macaroni
    (2 cups uncooked)

2 cups your favorite frozen vegetables,
    thawed and drained

1 6½-ounce can tuna, drained and flaked,
    or 1 6-ounce can chunk chicken

1 4-ounce package shredded cheddar cheese
    (about 1 cup)

¼ cup sweet pickle relish

½ cup mayonnaise

½ cup sour cream

1 tablespoon lemon juice

1 teaspoon instant minced onion

½ teaspoon salt

¼ teaspoon pepper

An adult should assist in preparing and draining elbow
macaroni according to package directions. In large bowl,
combine cooked macaroni, vegetables, tuna, cheese, and
pickle relish. In small bowl, blend remaining ingredients.
Add to macaroni mixture and mix well until coated.
Cover and store in refrigerator until cold. Stir gently
before serving. Makes 6 to 8 servings.

When the pasta salad has cooled, it's time to sit down and eat! The pasta has come a long way from the wheat fields to the kitchen table. It's good for you, and it tastes good, too. No matter what kind of pasta you eat—from spaghetti to macaroni, from spirals to shells—it may taste even better now that you know how pasta is made!